GREATEST
MOVIE
MONSTERS

MAR

ROBOTS AN CYBORGS

DAVID KASSNOFF

rosen publishing's
rosen
central®

D1225372

Published in 2016 by The Rosen Publishing Group, Inc.
29 East 21st Street, New York, NY 10010

First Edition

Library of Congress Cataloging-in-Publication Data

Kassnoff, David.
Robots and cyborgs/David Kassnoff.
    pages cm.—(Greatest movie monsters)
Includes bibliographical references and index.
ISBN 978-1-4994-3529-0 (library bound) — ISBN 978-1-4994-3530-6 (pbk.) — ISBN 978-1-4994-3532-0 (6-pack)
1. Cyborgs in motion pictures—Juvenile literature. 2. Transformers (Fictitious characters)—Juvenile literature. 3. Robots in motion pictures—Juvenile literature.
I. Title.
PN1995.9.C9K37 2016
791.43'675—dc23

2014047667

Manufactured in the United States of America

On the cover: The decepticon Megatron, from the 2007 movie *Transformers*.

CONTENTS

CHAPTER 1

MECHANICAL MEN, METROPOLIS, AND MORE

Robots are not built to be evil. At least, not in the real world. Today's robots walk, crawl, reach, and roll, performing simple and complex tasks in factories and in homes. They move objects, assemble parts, and even vacuum up dust. Today's cars are built by automated robot-like devices on high-tech assembly lines.

However, the robots in movies and TV shows often go haywire. To keep us entertained, these robots and more human-looking androids have quirky behavior or even turn on their creators. Robots first began to

Robots perform essential functions on most automobile assembly lines, freeing human workers to perform other needed tasks.

appear in feature films in the 1920s, and they are ever present in today's science fiction movies and shows. But the idea of creating a "living" servant to help mankind goes back thousands of years.

BEGINNINGS IN FOLK TALES

Both Greek and Jewish folklore talk about "living statues" that came to life to help their human masters, long before civilization had the ability to assemble complicated mechanical beings. The Jewish Talmud, a collection of stories and commentary about Jewish history, describes a golem—a living statue of clay that helps protect Jews from their enemies. However, none of these artificial creatures are really the same as the mechanical figures we know today. The creature imagined in Mary Shelley's *Frankenstein*, written in 1818, is not technically a robot or cyborg either, but he is assembled from human body parts and reanimated through the efforts of scientist Victor Frankenstein.

Today's movie fans think of robots as helpful mechanical servants. But the word "robot" has its roots in the idea of slavery, not service. Inspired by the Czech word for slave labor, *robota*, "robot" was first used in the 1920 play *R.U.R.* (short for *Rossum's Universal Robots*).

In writer Karel Capek's play, robots created for factory work and military service revolt, and nearly everyone perishes. The idea of robot servants becoming powerful and defying their creators has continued to be a theme in film and television for almost one hundred years.

The 1927 German film Metropolis *introduced the first female robot, called Maria, whose likeness copies that of the movie's female heroine.*

THE FIRST ROBOTS ON FILM

The first on-screen robots appeared in silent movies from Europe. In *The Mechanical Man* (1921), a giant robot terrorizes a city until a second mechanical man confronts the robot in a fight at a local opera house. Fritz Lang's *Metropolis* (1927) gives viewers an evil and alluring feminine robot patterned after the pacifist heroine Maria.

The robot incites a violent riot that nearly destroys the city.

When robots arrived in talkies, they were often assistants and henchmen of the main characters. At a time when an afternoon at the movies cost only a dime, Ming the Merciless, emperor of the planet Mongo, used robot soldiers called Annihilants in *Flash Gordon Conquers the Universe* (1940).

ROBOTS HAVE RULES

Legendary science fiction author Isaac Asimov created his Three Laws of Robotics in a short story published in 1942. This was years before he published the famous short story collection *I, Robot*, in 1950, and decades before *I, Robot* became popular again as a 2004 movie starring Will Smith and Bridget Moynihan. The three laws state:

1. A robot may not injure a human being or, through inaction, allow a human being to come to harm.
2. A robot must obey orders given it by human beings except where such orders would conflict with the First Law.
3. A robot must protect its own existence as long as such protection does not conflict with the First or Second Law.

Servant robots also appeared in a short 1941 Superman film and as the killer robot in *Mysterious Doctor Satan* (1940). Most of this era's robots were controlled by villains and did not think independently.

POSTWAR PERFORMERS

This portrayal of robots changed by the 1950s, when post–World War II America grew wary of possible Communist threats. Hollywood filmmakers manifested those fears in the form of powerful robots that displayed a limited ability to think independently. These robots—more allies than servants—added a sense of menace or mystery to sometimes peaceful-looking challengers.

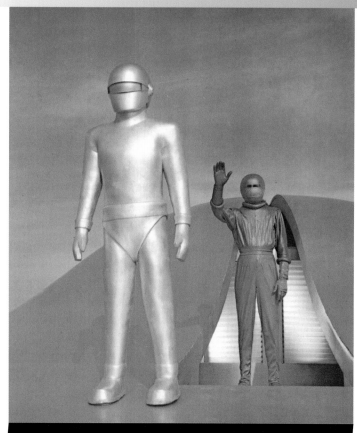

A giant 8-foot-tall (2.5 meter) robot with destructive laser-like vision, Gort helped create a sense of fear and uncertainty in 1951's **The Day the Earth Stood Still.**

A fascinating example of a "smart robot" is the giant Gort, the mechanical counterpart to the human-looking Klaatu in 1951's *The Day the Earth Stood Still*. Gort is the protector, and later the enforcer, of Klaatu's antiatomic weapon edict. After Klaatu arrives on Earth and is attacked, Gort defends their ship with powerful heat rays that destroy tanks and artillery. While Klaatu recovers and adopts a human lifestyle, Gort and similar police robots help enforce Klaatu's will on humanity.

In *Tobor the Great* (1954), the robot is less menacing and displays human emotions. The robot, designed for deep-space missions, is befriended by its inventor's eleven-year-old grandson. Tobor is later kidnapped by Communist agents who try to use Tobor against the United States. (In 1957, Tobor was reintroduced in a half-hour TV series, *Here Comes Tobor*, that was unsuccessful.)

Movie serials declined in the 1950s, but robots lived on. The robot from 1940's *Mysterious Doctor Satan* reappeared in a twelve-chapter serial, *Zombies of the Stratosphere* (1952). This practice of recycling robots in movies and TV series gave an unusually long lifespan to Robby the Robot, created for the 1956 science fiction classic *Forbidden Planet*.

ALONG CAME ROBBY

A futuristic version of William Shakespeare's *The Tempest*, *Forbidden Planet* introduced Robby as the mechanical alter ego of mysterious Dr. Morbius. Robby acted as Morbius's servant and protector. He later short-circuited himself while defending the film's main characters. He is revived at the end of the film to help pilot the heroes' escaping C-57D space cruiser.

The 7-foot-tall (2.1 m) Robby proved very popular with young film fans. He reappeared in 1957's *The Invisible Boy*. Later on, Robby popped up in a variety of TV series and movies in the 1960s and 1970s, including *The Man from U.N.C.L.E.*, *Lost in Space* (whose own Jupiter II robot shares some of Robby's design features), the detective series *Columbo*, the sci-fi comedy *Mork and Mindy*, and sitcoms such as *Hazel*, *The Addams Family*, and *The Monkees*.

Over a twenty-three-year career, Robby also outlived his creators. The original Robby prop suit has been rebuilt over time

Robby the Robot first appeared in 1956's Forbidden Planet *and went on to appear in movies and on TV for more than two decades.*

by a private collector, but the costume and its replicas continue to be popular attractions. Today, the EPM Museum in Seattle, Washington, and the Metreon complex in San Francisco, California, both exhibit Robby the Robot suits. Die-cast toys, plastic model kits, and other variations are sold online.

While Robby the Robot successfully rode the youth wave into the 1960s, other robots enjoyed less success. There were a few exceptions, though. The 1960s spy spoof *Get Smart!* featured an expressionless human-looking robot named Hymie, played by actor Dick Gautier. A transparent robot called Robert was a crewmember on the British TV series *Fireball XL5*, which aired in the United States from 1963 to 1965. Robots appeared in animated TV series, such as the robot maid Rosie on *The Jetsons* and as remote-controlled enemies in *Jonny Quest*.

MORE ROBOTS IN SPACE

Robots appeared in several episodes of the original *Star Trek* TV series but not as regular cast members. In the episode "The Doomsday Machine," the *Enterprise* confronts a giant automated space robot that destroys entire planets. Androids (self-guided robots capable of independent thought) are both allies and adversaries in "What Are Little Girls Made Of?" In "The Changeling," the crew encounters Nomad, a robotic space probe that threatens all life on the ship. In its second season, *Star Trek* devoted a full episode, "I, Mudd," to a planet inhabited by androids. In a third-season episode, "Requiem for Methuselah," the *Enterprise* crew meets a beautiful woman named Rayna on a remote planet; the captain falls in love with her, only to discover she is the latest in a long line of Rayna androids.

The original *Doctor Who* series, a British Broadcasting Corporation (BBC) program, featured mechanically encased beings called Daleks, who are actually cyborgs (see chapter 3), as well as a robot dog, K-9. On the big screen, however, most robots were used as comic relief or clumsy henchmen. Movies featuring robots that fall into this category include *Invasion of the Neptune Men* (1961), *Jason and the Argonauts* (1963), *Santa Claus Conquers the Martians* (1964), *Cyborg 2087* (1966), and *King Kong Escapes* (1967), which featured a robotic giant ape called Mechani-Kong.

CHAPTER 2

THE 1970s AND BEYOND: DISNEY, *STAR WARS*, AND DATA

Robots, cyborgs, and androids became major characters of films and TV series in the 1970s, 1980s, and beyond. They began to drive the plot, rather than support it. Viewers saw robot police in *THX 1138*, George Lucas's 1970 directorial debut. In *Silent Running* (1971), three amusing robot gardeners—named Huey, Dewey, and Louie—help Bruce Dern's character protect Earth's remaining plant life in space. Actor Yul Brynner played a menacing, out-of-control Western-style gunslinger robot in two sci-fi features, *Westworld* (1973) and *Futureworld* (1976).

Then, a film came along that changed every view of how robots could function. *Star Wars* (1977, later known as *Star Wars Episode IV: A New Hope*) catapulted two amusing sidekick robots, C-3PO and R2-D2, to the status of wildly popular, iconic characters.

A GALAXY OF ROBOTS AND CYBORGS

Star Wars broke new ground in movies, and audiences loved it. Its special effects gave a fresh, futuristic update to classic movie routines, including aerial dogfights, sword play, and chase scenes. But the chatter of the whiny and reluctant C-3PO and the fearless yet nonverbal R2-D2 was like no robot dialogue seen before.

Of course, *Star Wars* was filled with all manner of robots and cyborgs. When Uncle Owen selects a robot for his farm, his

Star Wars, *released in 1977, introduced C-3PO (left) and R2-D2 (right). The two lovable droids became wildly popular with fans. Both were based on artwork by Ralph McQuarrie.*

first choice isn't R2-D2, but a red robot with a "bad motivator." The Jawas, merchants of these captured robots, travel in a giant robotic land crawler. Mouse-like robots scurry through the corridors of the Death Star, the Empire's space station.

R2-D2 and C-3PO think and act more independently than previous movie robots. They argue with each other. They go off in different directions when they disagree. They work to fool the storm troopers searching for Luke and Han on the Death Star. They are fully developed, stand-alone characters, rather than mere sidekicks to the movie's heroes: Luke, Leia, and Han.

As episodes of the *Star Wars* series unfold, we learn more about their galaxy through the eyes of R2-D2 and C-3PO. Even after the first three *Star Wars* features, the robotic duo reappear as the common thread in 1999's *Star Wars Episode I: The*

IT'S HARD TO BE A ROBOT

When filming the *Star Wars* movies, actor Kenny Baker inhabited the can-like suit of R2-D2, while Anthony Daniels wore the golden cladding of C-3PO. Neither knew exactly what they faced when they began shooting *Star Wars*. Daniels, wearing C-3PO's metal suit, was unable to sit down in a chair in the hot desert sun. He could recline only on an uncomfortable leaning board. Baker, while working inside the R2-D2 prop suit, couldn't see the other robots—some on wires, others radio controlled—moving around him. One of the remote robots crashed into Baker's R2-D2 and tipped him over. Turtle like, he couldn't get up without help.

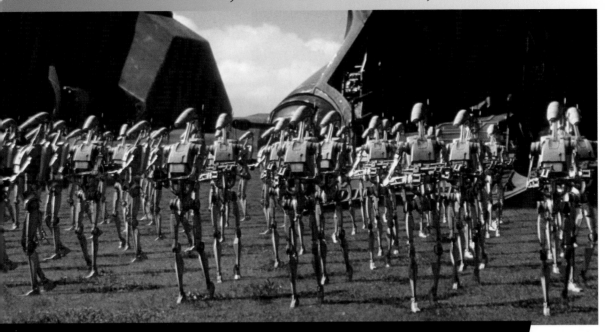

In 1999, Star Wars Episode I: The Phantom Menace—the first installment of a new Star Wars trilogy—introduced moviegoers to armies of battle droids during the Battle of Naboo.

Phantom Menace through 2015's *Star Wars Episode VII: The Force Awakens*.

FROM FILM TO TV AND BACK

The impact of *Star Wars* drove many movie studios to take a fresh look at science fiction. In 1979, the Walt Disney Company produced *The Black Hole*, featuring the evil robot Maximilian, who leads mechanized humanoids. Paramount Pictures scrambled to rework its 1960s TV series *Star Trek* for the big screen. The result was 1979's *Star Trek: The Motion Picture*, which featured two robotic characters: a giant, cloud-shielded V'Ger robot returning to Earth

Lt. Commander Data, played by actor Brent Spiner, became the first android crew member regularly featured in a Star Trek *series, starting with 1987's* Star Trek: The Next Generation.

to contact its creator and the human-like Ilia probe that merges with Captain Decker.

Aside from an occasional android adversary, *Star Trek* the TV series did not include a continuing robot or android character until 1987, when *Star Trek: The Next Generation* introduced viewers to Lieutenant Commander Data, an android serving as the second officer of the starship *Enterprise*.

What's the difference between an android and a robot? In most films and TV shows, androids are portrayed as superior to robots, able to analyze a situation and reason their way to a decision or action. This differs from most robots, whose actions are dictated solely by their programming. Data often found himself in situations where his actions defied his captain's orders and Starfleet regulations.

During the series, the character Lore—a kind of evil twin precursor to Data—was introduced and appeared in several episodes. In 1994, Data and the *Next Generation* crew moved to the big screen, appearing in *Star Trek: Generations* and in three more movies after that: *Star Trek: First Contact* (1996), *Star Trek: Insurrection* (1998), and *Star Trek: Nemesis* (2002). Prominently featured in these films, the Data character and his surviving android brother, B-4, were portrayed by actor Brent Spiner.

Another TV robot enjoyed a brief return to the movies in 1998 when a big-screen version of the 1960s series *Lost in Space* featured a version of the ship's original friendly robot, B-9. As in the TV series, this robot was voiced by the actor Dick Tufeld.

Some U.S. TV series featuring robots also found their way to movie screens—although not in the United States. *Battlestar Galactica* (1978) and *Buck Rogers in the 25th Century* (1979) both featured robotic characters. *Battlestar Galactica's* fierce adversaries were robotic warriors called Cylons. The two-hour pilot episodes of both series—minus commercials—were edited and shown to movie audiences in theatres outside the United States. In 2003, the Cylons reappeared as fearsome Centurion warriors in updated form in the reimagined *Battlestar Galactica* shown on the SYFY cable TV network.

TODAY'S ROBOTS

Sometimes robots acquire human traits, as in *Short Circuit*, a 1986 sci-fi comedy. In this film, a military robot named

Number 5 gains enough artificial intelligence to interact with the outside world—with comedic results.

Today, robots are widely used in feature films, sometimes appearing as characters with both human and robotic features. Such robots include Johnny Cab in *Total Recall* (1990), Alsatia Zevo in *Toys* (1992), SID 6.7 in *Virtuosity* (1995), Ash aboard the spaceship *Nostromo* in *Alien* (1999), the fembots in the *Austin Powers* movies, the battle droids in episodes I, II, and III of the *Star Wars* movies, Sonny and all the robots in *I, Robot* (2004), and the sentinels in *The Matrix* (1999) and its sequels.

Director Steven Spielberg explored the idea of a robot child looking for his place in a futuristic world in 2001's *A.I. Artificial Intelligence*. In a society in which mechanical robots interact with humans, the eleven-year-old David robot (played by actor Haley Joel Osment) is realistically human and capable of loving his adopted family. But, like Pinocchio, he is not a real boy.

Robots are among the main characters in the animated *The Iron Giant* (1999). *WALL-E* (2007) features the title character and a dozen other mechanical beings. RoboGadget in *Inspector Gadget* (1999) was a robotic version of Matthew Broderick's heroic inspector. Actor Robin Williams was one of many actors—including Ewan McGregor, Halle Berry, Greg Kinnear, Mel Brooks, Amanda Bynes, and Drew Carey—portraying characters in 2005's fully animated *Robots*.

WALL-E, *a 2007 feature film, gave us a lonely garbage-collecting robot toiling on an abandoned Earth who helps rescue mankind.*

The 2011 movie *Real Steel* was based on a 1963 episode of the popular *Twilight Zone* TV series. In *Real Steel*, a former prize fighter assembles a high-tech boxing robot from junk parts to compete in the boxing ring, where combat robots have replaced human boxers. The fighter's road to redemption is told through the metaphor of restoring the robot to fighting condition. Hugh Jackman stars as Charlie Kenton, who works with his young son Max to build and train their combat robot.

The 2014 computer-animated film *Big Hero 6* featured a downright heroic robot. This was an inflatable, lovable droid

ROBOT THAT'S ALL TOO HUMAN

While Oscar-winning comedic actor Robin Williams provided the voice to many animated robots and characters, his 1999 film *Bicentennial Man* showed a very different side of robots. Williams portrays a robot servant named Andrew who becomes a member of the family he serves. The film explores the advanced robot's two-hundred-year journey to become a compassionate, loving human. It deals with serious issues, including slavery, prejudice, growing older, and mortality. The science fiction comedy/family drama is based on the 1992 novel *The Positronic Man*, written by science fiction authors Isaac Asimov and Robert Silverberg.

Positronic brains show up in several of Asimov's robot stories. These computing devices serve as robots' artificial brains. Exactly how they work isn't fully explained, but they were the source of Asimov's robots' consciousness. The word "positronic" refers to the positron, a subatomic particle that is the antimatter pair to the more familiar electron.

The notion of a robot becoming human, as well as the idea of a positronic brain, also found its way to the character of Lieutenant Commander Data in *Star Trek: The Next Generation* and its four feature spin-off films.

called Baymax, who performed difficult tasks and protected his human friends. He also gathered his share of the laughs!

Filmmakers often use robots to help introduce plot devices and ideas that human actors cannot express. Robots can also provide comic subplots to science fiction films filled with action and combat. Robots will almost certainly be an ongoing staple in movies and TV series.

CYBORGS: MAN MEETS MACHINE

There's some confusion about what makes a cyborg. The word itself sounds scary, but it's just a combination of two different elements. The first part comes from cybernetics, the technology of using electronics to help control brain functions and nervous system functions. The "-org" element comes from the word "organism." A cyborg is most often a kind of mechanized and enhanced human, with strengths and abilities that exceed those of ordinary people.

In the real world, we know of at least one person who could be considered a cyborg. A British man named Kevin Warwick has a surgically implanted electronic device that links his nervous system with a computer network. Warwick is a professor of cybernetics at the University of Reading, in England. In August 1998, surgeons implanted a silicon chip transponder—a tiny radio link between Warwick and a computer network—in his left forearm. With this implant, a computer can follow Warwick through halls and offices in his university building. The chip also enables him to activate other electrical and electronic devices linked to the network remotely.

Like Warwick—who researches artificial intelligence, robotics, and related subjects—most fictional cyborgs have the ability to think and act independently. This is different from most robots, whose behavior is generally programmed into them by their creators.

BIONICS AND CONFLICT

Most successful movies deal with some kind of conflict between right and wrong or between good and evil. Cyborgs in motion pictures are usually human beings with mechanical or bionic implants or limbs that give them superhuman strength and abilities—often the ability to save lives or wreak havoc. In *I, Robot*, Will Smith plays a police detective investigating an executive's murder that may have been caused by one of the company's robots. Del Spooner, Smith's character, is a conflicted character; he hates robots but is a little bit of a cyborg himself—one of his arms is a bionic replacement.

Darth Vader, one of the most famous (and infamous) characters in all of science fiction, is actually a cyborg. After all, the former Anakin Skywalker is a human who was enhanced with robotic implants and limbs following his harrowing battle with Obi-wan Kenobi in *Star Wars Episode III: Revenge of the Sith* (2005). In fact, Anakin already had a prosthetic arm after losing

Will Smith plays a conflicted police detective fighting a corporate army of robots in I, Robot, *a 2004 film based on author Isaac Asimov's 1950 collection of short stories.*

his right one in a battle during *Star Wars Episode II: Attack of the Clones*. This echoes the prosthetic arm that his son Luke gets in *The Empire Strikes Back*.

WHO'S THE FIRST CYBORG?

In books and movies, the first mention of cyborgs as a melding of man and machine took place around 1960. A pilot and writer named Martin Caidin wrote a novel, *Cyborg*, in 1972. The book describes an American astronaut and test pilot named Steve

Austin who is horribly injured in the crash of a test aircraft. He is rebuilt with atomic-powered artificial legs and a bionic arm. He is also given sophisticated hearing and an enhanced "super eye." Austin goes on to become an agent for a government intelligence agency.

Caidin's cyborg-hero character became the hero of TV's popular *Six Million Dollar Man*, an action-adventure series starring Lee Majors as Austin that aired from 1973 until 1978. Caidin wrote several more novels featuring the Steve Austin character. ABC created a spin-off series, *The Bionic Woman* (1976–78), that featured actress Lindsey Wagner as Jaime Sommers, the first female cyborg with similar superpowered limbs and implants. After both TV series and several made-for-TV movies, Steve Austin and Jaime Sommers married in their final adventure, 1994's *Bionic Ever After?*

Caidin's characters keep resurfacing, however. In 2007, a reimagined *Bionic Woman* TV series starring British actress Michelle Ryan aired. The actor Mark Wahlberg steps into Steve Austin's flight suit in an update of Caidin's original story that features a higher price tag: *The Six Billion Dollar Man* in 2016.

Another famous cyborg is the Terminator. Arnold Schwarzenegger's robot-like marauder/guardian angel character functions with both mechanical and biological parts. The story begins with *The Terminator* (1984) and continues in 1991's *Terminator 2: Judgment Day* (which featured a liquid-metal adversary terminator), 2003's *Terminator 3: Rise of the Machines*, and 2009's *Terminator Salvation*, in which

"I'll be back" is a recurring phrase in a series of science fiction movies starring actor Arnold Schwarzenegger as the original Terminator cyborg.

Schwarzenegger's computer-generated likeness and stand-ins are used in scenes chronicling the creation of the T-101 terminator cyborg.

CYBORGS WE LOVE

Since cyborgs are generally long-lived, it seems fitting that they keep coming back to entertain us. While not all human/cybernetic characters are referred to as cyborgs on screen, we can still classify them as such.

INTRODUCING *ROBOCOP*

Among the best-known cyborgs is the title character of *RoboCop*, in which a critically injured Detroit police detective is rebuilt with armor, artificial limbs, and built-in weaponry—but a faulty memory—to fight crime. RoboCop debuted on the big screen in 1987. Actor Peter Weller originated the Alex Murphy/RoboCop character and played him again in *RoboCop 2* (1990). In 1993's *RoboCop 3*, the hero cyborg was played by actor Robert Burke.

The character later migrated to TV in a four-episode *RoboCop* miniseries, as well as to a series of video games. More recently, filmmakers revived the original character and story in 2014's *RoboCop*. Several series of Marvel comic books and two animated TV series have also chronicled RoboCop's ongoing adventures.

One famed hero who predates the use of the word "cyborg" but could be considered one is Iron Man. Comic book creator Stan Lee launched Iron Man as a Marvel Comics character in 1963. Iron Man starts as a normal man, industrialist Tony Stark, who creates for himself a life-saving reactor and armored flying suit. Iron Man became a popular hero in comic books and a 1990s animated TV series (*The Marvel Action Hour*). The character acquired advanced electronics in his armor that increased his abilities in 2008's *Iron Man*, starring actor Robert Downey Jr., who added his own wit and charm to the superhero's enhancements.

Iron Man, like many Marvel heroes, is a tormented character. In the 2008 film, he's given great powers through his technological implants. But Tony Stark is frustrated by the lethal results of the

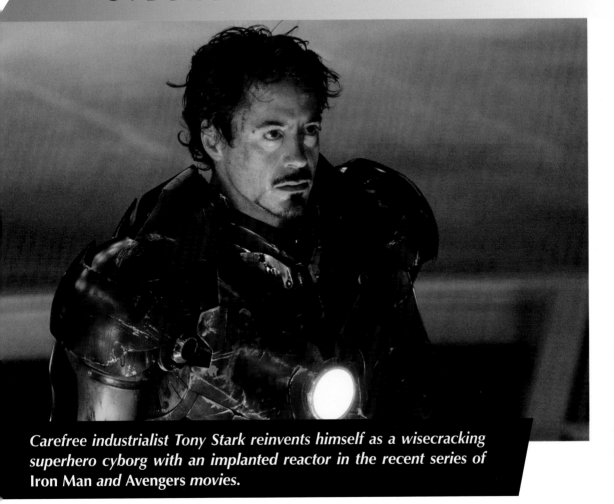

Carefree industrialist Tony Stark reinvents himself as a wisecracking superhero cyborg with an implanted reactor in the recent series of Iron Man *and* Avengers *movies.*

weapons manufacturing business his family has created, and his business partner later betrays him. *Iron Man 2*, released in 2010, shows a weakened Iron Man fighting to defend his father's legacy. In 2013's *Iron Man 3*, the character seeks revenge for an attack on his loved ones. The character is more brash and self-assured in Marvel's *Avengers* films: 2012's *The Avengers* and the 2015 release, *Avengers: Age of Ultron*.

Another cyborg in the Marvel universe appears in *Spider-Man 2*. Doctor Octopus, also known as Doc Ock, has octopus-like artificial limbs that, at least at first, are controlled by his mind. Not to be outdone, the DC Comics universe has its own superhuman/cyborg character: Cyborg, a.k.a. Victor Stone. Cyborg has appeared in *Teen Titans* and *Justice League* comics and animated films since his creation in 1980. A version of the character appeared in episodes of the *Smallville* TV series in the mid-2000s.

EVIL AND NOT-SO-EVIL CYBORGS

Cyborgs have made compelling film villains for decades. Among the earliest well-known evil cyborgs are the replicants of 1982's *Blade Runner*: the murderous Roy Batty, seductive Pris, fugitive Leon Kowalski, and Zhora, the exotic dancer replicant. Another advanced replicant, Rachael, becomes the love interest of the detective hero, Rick Deckard, played by Harrison Ford.

In the reimagined *Battlestar Galactica* (2003–2009), it's slowly revealed that some of the central characters are in fact next-generation Cylons, much more advanced than their robotic Centurion brothers. While human in appearance, they are synthetically created people. They include several *Galactica* crew members, including Lieutenant Boomer, Colonel Tigh, Sam Anders, and Chief Tyrol. The human-looking Cylons in direct combat with the Colonial crew members include Number One/Cavil, Number Two/Conoy, Number Three/D'Anna, and Number Six.

The long-running British TV program *Doctor Who* began as a low-budget science-fiction series. In need of a threatening species, the series creators introduced the Daleks in 1963. These mutated alien creatures exist in armored time-travel machines, and their external structure includes a mechanical eye set in a rotating dome, a manipulator arm, and a gun-like device protruding from the Dalek body. The creatures often shout "Exterminate!" or "Destroy!" in the series' combat scenes.

Cybermen **(left)** *and Daleks* **(right)** *have recurred several times throughout the over fifty-year run of the BBC's wildly popular sci-fi TV series* **Doctor Who.**

In 1966, the Doctor first confronted Cybermen. These robotic creatures owed much of their early armor-like appearance to the Tin Man in *The Wizard of Oz*. Cybermen appeared less frequently than Daleks on *Doctor Who*; when they returned in 2011, they owed much of their updated appearance to Iron Man and the Imperial stormtroopers of *Star Wars*. While Cybermen may look like robots, they are actually cyborgs. In the original *Doctor Who*, they came into being when human-like beings from the planet Mondas started replacing parts of their bodies in order to better survive. The revived version of the show featured Cybermen who originated as human beings.

The various *Star Trek* TV series have their own cyborgs, too. In *Star Trek: The Next Generation*, the Borg are introduced as a menacing collective of humanoids implanted with cybernetics. After appearing in several episodes (including "I, Borg" and the two-part "The Best of Both Worlds") and the spin-off series *Star Trek: Voyager*, the Borg emerge as the main adversary in the eighth Star Trek theatrical film, *Star Trek: First Contact* (1996). In *Voyager*, the rescued female Borg, Seven of Nine (played by Jeri Ryan), becomes a member of the ship's crew in the series' second season.

CHAPTER 4

TRANSFORMERS NOW AND THEN

In 1984, the toy and game company Hasbro Inc.—creators of G.I. Joe—wanted a new kind of shape-changing action figure toy, so the company went to Japan to license many converting toys that looked like robots. Taken together, these toys were marketed as the Transformers, a set of twenty-one action figures. The original Transformers converted from trucks and other vehicles to powerful-looking combat robots.

To promote the toy line, Hasbro cocreated the original animated TV series *Transformers* in 1984. The series used the refrain "robots in disguise" in its theme song, but the Transformers were dramatically different from any robots or cyborgs seen in other TV shows or feature films.

Unlike preprogrammed robots or cybernetically enhanced humans, the Transformers—inhabitants of a fully mechanized planet, Cybertron—are a distinct species with great strength and the ability to make moral choices and form alliances with other species, including humans. They can also convert from towering mechanized warriors to automobiles, aircraft, trucks, and more.

TRANSFORMERS MYTHOLOGY

The first generation of Transformers found their way to an animated action TV series featuring the familiar characters we know today. These included Bumblebee, Jazz, Starscream, the lordly and ultrapowerful Optimus Prime, and the power-mad

Bumblebee's first incarnation as a Transformer was as an action figure, before leaping to the TV screen and, later, to the movie multiplex.

Megatron. The popularity of both the toys and the animated Saturday morning TV series led the characters to a feature-length animated movie in 1986.

Transformers mythology begins on the planet Cybertron. There, two groups of Transformers—the Autobots and the Decepticons—battled for control of the ultimate source of power in the universe, called the AllSpark. Covered with strange alien symbols, the cube-like Allspark was said to regulate the planet's internal currents and help keep it safe. Megatron, Cybertron's Lord High Protector, launched a planet-wide civil war when he tried to claim the AllSpark as his own.

The 28-foot-tall (8.5 m) Optimus Prime leads the Autobot troops against Megatron's Decepticon forces. To keep the AllSpark from falling into Megatron's metallic hands, Optimus Prime launches the cube into deep space. The AllSpark's course changes unexpectedly, though, sending it toward Earth, where the Autobots and Decepticons continue their fierce conflict.

In the original TV series, Optimus Prime's beginnings were humble. A worker robot known as Orion Pax, he was created by an alien race called the Quintessence millions of years before the current Transformers timeline. Later, Optimus led an expedition to search for new sources of energy in a space vessel called the *Ark*, pursued by Megatron's own space ship, *Nemesis*. Both ships crash-landed on Earth, and the Autobots and Decepticons lay hidden and undiscovered for thousands of years until they were reawakened by an erupting volcano.

What comes next may surprise fans of the current *Transformers* movies. In *The Transformers: The Movie* (1986), the brutal conflict results in the death of Optimus Prime. Fans loudly voiced their displeasure, and Hasbro and its filmmaking partners quickly revived Optimus Prime for the continuing (1984–1987) animated TV series, as well as later versions to follow.

POWER TO TRANSFORM

Autobots and Decepticons can change into a variety of different vehicles and devices. Optimus Prime becomes a red-flamed Peterbilt semi tractor-trailer in the first nonanimated *Transformers* feature film. Others can morph into flashy sports cars, military jeeps, or jet aircraft. Some become less striking objects, such as a large handgun or a 1980s-era boom box stereo—a skill less in demand in today's era of pocket-sized MP3 players and smartphones.

Later TV episodes introduced Constructicons, robot beings modeled after backhoes, bulldozers, dump trucks, and construction-site machinery. They combine to form gigantic combat machines, including one known as Devastator, a simple-minded machine that destroys anything in its path. Another subset includes Pretenders, who use living tissue to hide their real mechanical identities. Still other Transformers can adapt to work with a living organism, like a human pilot, and share consciousness in a single mind. Hasbro introduced ever-expanding action figure toys to coincide with these characters in its TV series.

One constant throughout the thirty-year Transformers history is Megatron, the leader of the marauding Decepticons. Megatron transforms into a fierce interstellar fighter jet that can travel soundlessly at about three times the speed of light. With strong defensive hull plates, Megatron's vehicle mode includes a powerful tractor beam that can immobilize approaching or fleeing combatants. In early versions, Megatron could also transform into a Walther P38 handgun that could be fired by other Decepticons at opponents—a function that at first worried Hasbro toy executives.

The ruthless Megatron towers at 35 feet (10.7 m) tall. He has a "dark matter" power core, which fuels his hundred-megawatt

THE NEXT VOICE WE HEAR

While animators worked to create an original universe of combat robots from the planet Cybertron, *The Transformers: The Movie* relied on a cast of well-known actors to supply voices to the Autobots and Decepticons. In the TV series, Peter Cullen had voiced Optimus Prime, while Frank Welker provided Megatron's voice. But producers of the film hired Leonard Nimoy (who played *Star Trek*'s Mr. Spock) to be the voice of Galvatron. Other notable actors in the 1986 film included Robert Stack (from *Airplane!*) as Ultra Magnus, Judd Nelson (from *The Breakfast Club*) as Hot Rod/Rodimus Prime, Orson Welles (from *Citizen Kane*) as Unicron, and Eric Idle (from *Monty Python and the Holy Grail*) as Wreck-Gar.

lightning emitters and shell cannons. He's also capable of self-repairing internal or external damage. In 1986's *The Transformers: The Movie*, Megatron was reformatted into an even stronger warrior called Galvatron.

BIG-SCREEN TRANSFORMERS

After some twenty years of small-screen animated adventures and video games featuring the Transformers, filmmakers agreed that computer-generated imagery (CGI) technology now made it possible to bring realistic Transformers to the cineplex. The result was *Transformers* (2007), an action-packed feature film that revived the Autobots' and Decepticons' battle for the All-Spark cube.

The film featured a number of humans to help narrate the action for a new generation of movie fans. Shia LaBeouf played Sam Witwicky, the young human caught in the ongoing battle. Other featured performers were Jon Voight as the U.S. secretary of defense and Megan Fox as Sam's girlfriend, Mikaela Banes. Veteran *Transformers* actor Peter Cullen brought his voice talent to the role of Optimus Prime. Actor Hugo Weaving—known for his roles in two science fiction movie trilogies, the *Matrix* franchise and *The Lord of the Rings*—became the voice of the evil Megatron.

There's also a little bit of *Star Wars* DNA in *Transformers*. The film's life-like robotic characters and visual effects were created by Industrial Light & Magic, the Lucasfilm-owned digital effects experts behind the high-tech realism in every

Starting in 2007, with each Transformers feature film, the heroic Optimus Prime appears more powerful as he morphs from Peterbilt semi tractor-trailer into the leader of the Autobots.

Star Wars film since 1977, as well as several *Star Trek* films and the *Back to the Future* movies.

The Transformers returned in 2009's *Transformers: Revenge of the Fallen*, which featured Sam Witwicky and Mikeala Banes again defending Earth from Decepticons alongside the Autobots. The film introduced a new foe, an evil Prime robot called the Fallen. *Transformers: Dark of the Moon* (2011) brought us the Autobots and Decepticons fighting over an alien technology hidden on Earth's moon. This third film marked the

Transformers: Dark of the Moon *saw robots fighting for an alien technology on the moon. Apollo 11 astronaut Buzz Aldrin—the second man to walk on the moon—appears in the film.*

last appearance of Shia LaBeouf's Sam Witwicky character. In 2014's *Transformers: Age of Extinction*, the action shifts to Texas, where an inventor named Cade Yeager (played by actor Mark Wahlberg) discovers a crippled Optimus Prime and helps him recover to fight the Decepticons as well as humans who've grown fearful of the Transformers on Earth.

ROBOTS IN TOMORROW'S FILMS

Today's entertainment industry knows that robots, cyborgs, and mechanized transformer-type beings are favorites for moviegoers. Audiences don't always buy how cyborgs, androids, and robots are portrayed, though. For example, in 2014, the TV series *Almost Human* paired actor Karl Urban as a police detective with actor Michael Ealy as his android partner. The series, cocreated by *Star Trek* film director J.J. Abrams, earned good reviews but weak viewer ratings. It was canceled after only a few months.

There's no perfect formula for success for a movie featuring robots. The *Transformers* movies feature relentless robot combat and explosions. The *Star Wars* films turn in part on the antics of two loveable robotic characters, R2-D2 and C-3PO. A lovelorn robot is the centerpiece of *WALL-E*. Most successful robot movies mix compassionate robots with mystery and conflict.

Robots and cyborgs continue to be popular, especially on the big screen. Big movie franchises have been particularly successful in recent years. Arnold Schwarzenegger's iconic

T-800 Terminator appears in 2015's *Terminator Genisys*, though he is not the only Terminator in the film. There are plans to release a fifth movie in the rebooted *Transformers* franchise in 2016. Iron Man makes another appearance in 2015's *Avengers: Age of Ultron*, while *Star Wars Episode VII: The Force Awakens* features both familiar and new robots.

Now it's up to a new generation of screenwriters, animators, and movie studios to look at today's scientific breakthroughs and create cyborgs and robots that reflect the most advanced melding of mind and machines. All robots and cyborgs, after all, begin as the creation of some writer's or engineer's imagination.

FILMOGRAPHY

The Day the Earth Stood Still (1951)
Director: Robert Wise
Actors: Michael Rennie, Patricia Neal, and Sam Jaffe

Forbidden Planet (1956)
Director: Fred M. Wilcox
Actors: Walter Pidgeon, Leslie Nielsen, Anne Francis, and Jack Kelly

THX 1138 (1970)
Director: George Lucas
Actors: Robert Duvall, Donald Pleasance, and Maggie McOmie.

Silent Running (1971)
Director: Douglas Trumbull
Actors: Bruce Dern, Cliff Potts, and Ron Rifkin

Westworld (1973)
Director: Michael Crichton.
Actors: Yul Brynner, Richard Benjamin, and James Brolin

Futureworld (1976)
Director: Richard T. Heffron
Actors: Yul Brynner, Peter Fonda, and Blythe Danner

Star Wars (1977)
Director: George Lucas
Actors: Harrison Ford, Mark Hamill, and Alec Guinness

The Black Hole (1979)
Director: Gary Nelson.
Actors: Robert Forster, Maximilian Schell, and Anthony Perkins

The Terminator (1984)
Director: James Cameron
Actors: Arnold Schwarzenegger, Linda Hamilton, and Michael Biehn

RoboCop (1987)
Director: Paul Verhoeven
Actors: Peter Weller, Nancy Allen, and Ronny Cox

Star Trek: First Contact (1996)
Director: Jonathan Frakes
Actors: Patrick Stewart, Brent Spiner, and James Cromwell

Transformers (2007)
Director: Michael Bay
Actors: Shia LaBeouf, Megan Fox, and Jon Voight

Iron Man (2008)
Director: Jon Favreau
Actors: Robert Downey Jr., Gwyneth Paltrow, and Jeff Bridges.

Terminator Salvation (2009)
Director: McG (Joseph McGinty Nichol)
Actors: Christian Bale and Sam Worthington

Transformers: Age of Extinction (2014)
Director: Michael Bay
Actors: Mark Wahlberg and Kelsey Grammer

Star Wars Episode VII: The Force Awakens (2015)
Director: J. J. Abrams
Actors: John Boyega, Daisy Ridley, and Oscar Isaac

GLOSSARY

ALLIANCE An agreement in which people, groups, or countries work together to reach a common goal.

ANDROID A human-looking robot able to make independent decisions.

AUTOMATION Making an object or system that can operate without direct control by a person.

BIONIC Having artificial body parts with electronic or mechanical parts.

COLLECTIVE A group in which all participants share in making decisions.

COMMUNIST Believing in a system in which all property is owned in common.

CYBERNETICS The science of communications and automatic control systems in machines and living organisms.

ELECTRONIC Powered by electricity, which is the flow of electrons.

HENCHMAN A trusted follower who caries out unpleasant, illegal, or immoral acts for a powerful boss.

IMPLANT A device or object that is surgically inserted or attached to a body's living tissue.

INTERSTELLAR Relating to travel or distances between star systems.

NERVOUS SYSTEM The brain and all the nerves in a living body that permit movement and feeling.

PACIFIST Believing in and promoting peace; antiwar.

REPLICA An exact or nearly exact copy of something.

SERIAL A story or sequence of films that appear in regular installments over many weeks.

SYNTHETIC Made from artificial substances.

TRANSPONDER A device that both sends out and receives signals, in particular radio signals.

FOR MORE INFORMATION

American Film Institute

2021 N. Western Avenue

Los Angeles, CA 90027

(323) 856-7600

Website: http://www.afi.com

The American Film Institute honors the heritage of the moving picture arts and educates filmmakers and students. It maintains a catalog of some sixty-thousand American-made feature films.

Canadian Film Institute (CFI)

2 Daly Avenue, Suite 120

Ottawa, ON K1N 6E2

Canada

(613) 232-6727

Website: http://www.cfi-icf.ca

CFI promotes the production, diffusion, study, appreciation, and use of moving images for cultural and educational purposes in Canada and abroad. CFI organizes public film programming, distributes films, and helps publish books on Canadian cinema.

Canadian Media Production Association (CMPA)

160 John Street, 5th Floor

Toronto, ON M5V 2E5

Canada

(416) 304-0280

Website: http://www.cmpa.ca

CMPA is a national nonprofit organization that works with more than 350 companies engaged in the production and distribution of television programs, feature films, and digital media content in Canada.

Science Fiction and Fantasy Writers of America (SFWA)

P.O. Box 3238

Enfield, CT 06083

Website: http://www.sfwa.org

SFWA is a membership organization of more than 1,700 commercially published writers of science fiction, fantasy, and related genres. Its membership includes writers of both stand-alone works and short fiction published with other works.

World Science Fiction Society (WSFS)

P.O. Box 426159

Kendall Square Station

Cambridge, MA 02142

Website: http://www.wsfs.org

WSFS selects recipients of the annual Hugo Awards (Science Fiction Achievement Awards). It also chooses locations and committees for the annual World Science Fiction Convention (Worldcons) and the occasional North American Science Fiction Convention.

WEBSITES

Because of the changing nature of Internet links, Rosen Publishing has developed an online list of websites related to the subject of this book. This site is updated regularly. Please use this link to access the list:

http://www.rosenlinks.com/GMM/Robot

FOR FURTHER READING

Asimov, Isaac. *I, Robot*. New York, NY: Bantam Spectra, 2008.

Aylett, Ruth. *Robots: Bringing Intelligent Machines to Life*. Hauppauge, NY: Quarto Publishing, 2002.

Barber, John. *Transformers: Robots in Disguise*. Vol. 6. San Diego, CA: IDW Publishing, 2014.

Furman, Simon. *Transformers: The Movie Guide*. New York, NY: DK Publishing, 2007.

Garcia, Frank, and Mark Phillips. *Science Fiction Television Series, 1990–2004: Histories, Casts and Credits for 58 Shows*. Jefferson, NC: McFarland, 2012.

Gerani, Gary. *Top 100 Sci-Fi Movies*. San Diego, CA: IDW Publishing, 2011.

Mann, George. *Doctor Who: Engines of War*. New York, NY: Broadway Books, 2014.

Nagle, Jeanne. *Great Authors of Science Fiction and Fantasy*. New York, NY: Britannica Educational Publishing, 2014.

Nathan, Ian. *Terminator Vault: The Complete Story Behind the Making of "The Terminator" and "Terminator 2: Judgment Day."* Hauppauge, NY: Voyageur Press/Quarto Publishing, 2013.

Perkowitz, Sidney. *Hollywood Science: Movies, Science, and the End of the World*. New York, NY: Columbia University Press, 2007.

Ruditis, Paul. *Star Trek: The Visual Dictionary*. New York, NY: DK Publishing, 2013.

Schneider, Steven Jay. *1001 Movies You Must See Before You Die*. 4th edition. Hauppauge, NY: Quintessence, 2011.

Whitby, Blay. *Artificial Intelligence*. New York, NY: Rosen Publishing, 2009.

BIBLIOGRAPHY

Brevet, Brad, "Transformers' Timeline: 1984-Present." *Rope of Silicon*, June 22, 2007. Retrieved November 20, 2014 (http://www.ropeofsilicon .com/transformers_timeline_1984_present).

Caidin, Martin. *Cyborg*. New York, NY: Arbor House Publishing, 1972.

"Flash Gordon Serials (1936)." Retrieved November 18, 2014 (http:// www.umich.edu/~engb415/film/Flash_Gordon_serials.html).

Furman, Simon. *Transformers: The Movie Guide*. New York, NY: DK Publishing, 2007.

Guggenheim.org. "The Mechanical Man by André Deed." Calendar & Events. Retrieved November 19, 2014 (http://www.guggenheim.org).

Hardy, Phil. *The Overlook Film Encyclopedia: Science Fiction*. Woodstock, NY: The Overlook Press, 1991.

Here Comes Tobor. "Failed Pilot—Tobor and the Atomic Submarine." 1957. Retrieved November 20, 2014 (https://archive.org/details/tobor01).

MIT Technology Review. "Do We Need Asimov's Laws?" May 16, 2014. Retrieved November 18, 2014 (http://www.technologyreview.com /view/527336/do-we-need-asimovs-laws).

Perkowitz, Sidney. *Hollywood Science: Movies, Science, and the End of the World*. New York, NY: Columbia University Press, 2007.

Rinzler, J. W. *The Making of Star Wars*. New York, NY: Del Ray Books/ Random House, 2007.

Schneider, Steven Jay. *1001 Movies You Must See Before You Die*. 4th edition. Hauppauge, NY: Quintessence, 2011.

University of Reading. "Professor Kevin Warwick: The Transponder." March 2002. Retrieved November 8, 2014 (http://www.kevinwarwick.com/ the_transponder.htm).

Warwick, Kevin. *I, Cyborg*. London, England: Century, 2002.

Zehr, E. Paul. *Inventing Iron Man: The Possibility of a Human Machine*. Baltimore, MD: The Johns Hopkins University Press, 2011.

INDEX

ABOUT THE AUTHOR

David Kassnoff is an author, writer, and educator with more than twenty years of experience working with information technology professionals and technologists. His writing has appeared in *American Biotechnology Laboratory*, *Diversity Executive*, *Profiles in Diversity Journal*, *USA Weekend*, *Audio-Visual Communications*, *Democrat and Chronicle* newspaper (Rochester, New York), *Photo Marketing*, *Rochester Business* magazine, the *Finger Lakes Times*, the *Los Angeles Times Magazine*, *Photo Trade News*, and *Practical Homeowner*. He teaches at the Russell J. Jandoli School of Journalism and Mass Communication at St. Bonaventure University. In 1977, he purchased an original *Star Trek* tribble and went to the theater to see the original *Star Wars: A New Hope*—seven times.

PHOTO CREDITS

Cover, pp. 6, 15 © Moviestore collection Ltd/Alamy; p. 4 Gerhard Joren/LightRocket/Getty Images; p. 8 Silver Screen Collection/Moviepix/Getty Images; p. 10 courtesy Everett Collection; p. 13 © Lucasfilm/courtesy Everett Collection; p. 16 CBS Photo Archive/Getty Images; p. 19 © Walt Disney Studios Motion Pictures/courtesy Everett Collection; pp. 23, 25, 27, 37 © AF archive/Alamy; p. 29 Photo by Chris Balcombe/Rex Features/courtesy Everett Collection; p. 32 © Sumod Sunny/Alamy; p. 38 © Photos 12/Alamy; p. 41 Andrey_Kuzmin/Shutterstock.com; interior pages banners and backgrounds Nik Merkulov/Shutterstock.com, Apostrophe/Shutterstock.com.

Designer: Brian Garvey; Editor: Amelie von Zumbusch